A Quitter's Little Instruction Book

First published 2003 by Boxtree
an imprint of Pan Macmillan Ltd
Pan Macmillan, 20 New Wharf Road, London N1 9RR
Basingstoke and Oxford
Associated companies throughout the world
www.panmacmillan.com

ISBN 0 7522 1566 3

9 8 7 6 5 4 3 2 1

A CIP catalogue record for this book is available from
the British Library.

Designed by Perfect Bound Ltd
Printed by the Bath Press Ltd

BUTT OUT!

A Quitter's Little Instruction Book

Mike Anderiesz

BOXTREE

CONTENTS

INTRODUCTION

Having smoked between five and twenty a day for many years, the question I ask myself most often is not how do I stop, but why the hell did I start?

The truth is, all the medical evidence in the world won't make a hint of difference unless you realize why you started, how little smoking has added to your life and how many things it will stop you doing in the future.

Most of Britain's thirteen million smokers began out of peer pressure, something they spend the rest of their lives denying. I did it because I wanted to look more important.

Fifteen years later my teeth don't look so good, I turn green if I have to run more than fifty yards and I don't enjoy food if I'm sitting in a no-smoking restaurant. Anyway, that's why I decided to quit and drag you along for the ride. Because if a man with no willpower and an apparent death wish can do it, you can do it too.

Well, maybe. By the time you read this I'll probably be smoking again. Statistically there's a 20 per cent chance of failure. That's not the point. The point is Quitting, in its own way, is as blissfully addictive as smoking. And I'm going to prove it.

DANGER
Carcinogen
Like you didn't know

Butt Out is a self-contained Quitting course. Simply follow the instructions at the end of each chapter and enjoy the bits in between, most of which are true. And if you usually have a fag right about now, go and light one up. In fact, I'm doing that right now. Mmmm.

There. Now enjoy it, because at the end of Chapter 2 we're going to stub it out.

CHAPTER 1

SO YOU THINK YOU WANT TO QUIT

The first step to Quitting is establishing how much of a die-hard smoker you really are.

There's nothing worse than enduring twelve weeks of expensive nicotine patches, frayed nerves and eating your own weight in doughnuts only to realize 'Hey, hang on … I didn't even smoke.'

So to help you test your level of addiction here's a simple self-assessment quiz – just tick anything that applies to you and then ask some bored receptionist to analyse the results, just like they do in glossy magazines. Ready?

You could get hit
by lightning?
Yeah, right. Sure

---

1) What is the first thing you do every morning?

a) Light a ciggy.

b) Stub one out (being unconscious is never an obstacle to the committed smoker).

c) Shave your tongue.

2) You are on a long-haul non-smoking flight. What do you do?

a) Ask if you can sit in the cockpit and get drunk with the pilot.

b) Hope you can sleep all the way till landing.

c) Devise an elaborate system for smoking in the toilet, involving taking long drags, running up the aisle and French-kissing a stewardess in order to exhale.

Go on. give it a go

---

3) It is 3 a.m., the shops are closed and you find yourself down to one fag. Do you:

a) Lick the bottom of the carton for every last shred of precious weed.

b) Split your last ciggy into sections and pace yourself till morning.

c) Drive round for hours looking for an all-night service station, then spend fifteen minutes miming 'Twenty Silk Cut, please' through sound-proof glass to some stoned seventeen-year old who failed the entrance exam at Burger King.

---

4) Your partner has a Persian cat called Pooh Manchu who is allergic to cigarette smoke. Do you:

a) Attempt to reason with your partner, arguing logically why a change of pet may be best for both of you.

b) Change your partner. There's plenty more fish in the sea.

c) Smoke the cat.

5) You are invited to dinner at a no-smoking restaurant. What do you do?

a) Make the ultimate sacrifice of not having your after-dinner ciggy.

b) Devise an elaborate system of inhaling in the lav and then running back and exhaling into your vol au vent.

c) Accuse the chef of eyeing up your girlfriend, pick a fight with him and drown him in his own lobster bisque – all so you can enjoy that ciggy in the back of the police car.

Quit it!

6) You are watching TV when one of those harrowing anti-smoking commercials comes on. Do you:

a) Change channels. No point depressing yourself.

b) Make some feeble attempt at humour … for example, watching it solemnly, saying, 'Makes you think, doesn't it?' and then cramming twenty ciggies into your mouth at once.

c) Break down in tears and refuse to stop until someone reassures you that the nasty TV man made up all that stuff about cancer.

You stink.
Sorry

---

7) Your office has a strict no-smoking policy. What do you do?

a) Live with it. Over 60 per cent of businesses now do the same.

b) Find a new job. It would interfere with your efficiency, anyway.

c) Devise an elaborate system for inhaling in the toilet and exhaling into a photocopier, filing cabinet or, at a push, your blouse or shirt. When someone points out that your tits appear to be on fire, smile seductively and say, 'If you think they're smoking, you should see my arse!'

---

8) You have finally pulled someone you really fancy and taken them back to your place. Do you:

a) Put on some light jazz, crack open a bottle of wine and dim the lights.

b) Put on a good movie and spend the next two hours trying to work out where to put your arm.

c) Say, 'Listen, why don't we just skip the foreplay, sex and mutual holding and go straight to the post-coital ciggy?'

Bye bye

---

9) Your doctor walks towards you holding some X-rays in one hand and a rosary in the other. He seems to be in tears. Do you:

a) Prepare yourself for bad news. What the heck, you had a good innings.

b) Prepare yourself for good news. The majority of cancers are now treatable and a positive attitude is always a good start.

c) Have a fag. In fact, offer the doctor one too.

Are you enjoying that ciggy? Good. Because it's nearly time to put it out.

CHAPTER 2

ALL IN THE MIND

Having failed the question-naire, you may suspect you have a problem, but this is only the start. Before you can Quit (bear with me, I don't get paid unless I complete the book!) you need to know exactly what your problem is.

What is it about smoking you like, need or crave, and how might it be replaced? Remember what George W. Bush said while forging his astronaut application form: 'All addiction is 63 per cent mental, 59 per cent physical and 23 per cent likely to end in military confrontation. Now leave me alone, I'm on the toilet.'

DANGER
Harmful fumes
and dog breath

Chemical

Tobacco smoke contains up to four hundred chemicals but we smoke mainly because of our addiction to just one, nicotine. Forget all that crap you talk about lifestyle choices and self-image – we're junkies and there's nothing we can do about it. Or is there? See Chapter 4 for a few painless alternatives.

Psychological

Freud thought cigarettes were a sign of oral fixation. Basically he believed that we smoke for the same reason we suck dummies or occasionally get busted in public lavatories with other men – not his best theory, perhaps, but it makes a change from blaming everything on his sodding mum.

You could get hit
by lightning?
Yeah, right. Sure

Sensual

Like any habit, smoking changes
our body language, with the act
of holding something in one hand
and putting it in your mouth
becoming as natural as blinking.
After quitting, you will certainly
miss this routine, so why not do
something that requires a similar
motor-function, such as becoming
a football referee, food taster or
prostitute?

Social

We never escape our childhood urge to blend in with the crowd. Consequently, if you hang out with smokers you will feel tempted to smoke. This is how kids get into it in the first place. Makes you wonder what's happening to kids today, doesn't it? Why aren't they out listening to gangsta rap or picking up adults on the Internet?

Aspirational

Sociologists and advertisers believe we all secretly want to be celebrities, and as most of them are inveterate smokers (*see Chapter 7*) some of that must be rubbing off on us. Almost all classic jazz or silent movies glamorize smoking by linking us to a time before it had sinister overtones. Ever see Humphrey Bogart lean over towards Ingrid Bergman and say, 'Here's coughing up phlegm, kid...'? Didn't think so.

Instinctual

This is the hardest form of addiction, because of its unpredictability. When you get stressed you feel a stronger need to smoke and so the cycle begins. As always it is best to approach such problems in an analytical fashion. For example: 'OK, so there's a problem with the marketing report and it's due tomorrow ... now, how will me dropping dead of emphysema at the age of forty help the situation?'

Narcissistic

The classic 'well, you've got to die somehow ... you could die crossing the road' argument – as repeated by morons and maniacs the world over. Using this argument is a bit like covering your genitals in honey, standing near a beehive and saying, 'Yes, but there's a 5 per cent chance the hypothermia will kill me first ... '

OK, stub out the ciggy and don't even think of lighting another till Chapter 7.

CHAPTER 3

25 COMPELLING REASONS TO QUIT

Now we've established you're a filthy beast in need of help, here are twenty-five reasons to quit while you have any semblance of willpower left.

1) You'll be able to run for a bus and not end up the same colour as one.

2)   If you're a Native American,
they won't call you 'Falls
Down Gasping', 'Big Chief
Yellow Fingers' or 'Dances
with Asthmatics'.

3) You'll realize that tongue
   sandwiches do not always
   taste stale.

4) You won't need to call out the
   AA to jump-start your heart
   on a cold morning.

5) You'll have more money to spend on beer; the drug of choice for people who need to feel better about themselves while vomiting at the same time.

6) You won't wake up tasting like a tramp urinated in your mouth. (NB: If you are a heavy drinker as well as a smoker, it's quite likely this actually happened the last time you passed out.)

DANGER
Harmful fumes
and dog breath

7) You'll be able to grin at a
mirror without thinking
'Argh!!! Fu Manchu!'

8) Your sex life will improve – for a start, partners can take the clothes pegs off their noses.

You could get hit by lightning? Yeah, right. Sure

9) People will not be able to tell your age by counting the rings under your eyes.

10) People won't be able to see or smell you 30 seconds before you enter a room.

11) You won't have to apologize for finishing this year's London Marathon early next year ... ten minutes after the guy in the rabbit suit.

12) When meeting chic friends
you don't have to defend
carrying twenty Marlboro
Lights as your one fashion
accessory.

13) You can take out life insurance
without having to lie about
everything except your sexual
orientation.

14) You won't keep seeing
mysterious figures carrying
scythes lurking in the
shadows.

15) You can plan for your retirement without having to make extra allowances for oxygen tanks and private nurses. Mind you, private nurses seem to be advertising in phone boxes these days, so what the hell.

16) When the grandchildren come round you don't have to avoid the tricky subject of 'where Grampa wants his ashes dumped'.

You stink.
Sorry

17) Songs like 'Smoke Gets In Your Eyes', 'Killing Me Softly' and 'Seasons in the Sun' won't make you depressed. Well, except the last one – if you can find an uplifting meaning to 'Goodbye, my friends, it's hard to die, when all the birds are singing in the sky' treat yourself to a ciggy at once!

18) You don't have to find excuses
for disconnecting the TV or
going temporarily deaf on
National No-Smoking Day.

19) You'll have a better excuse for being late than 'Sorry ... I was coughing up blood on the Northern line.'

DANGER cheap lighters

20) You can look forward to New Year's Day without having to make Quitting one of your resolutions. Now it's just the easy stuff like 'Must stop talking crap in pubs' and 'Must make something of my life before the kids disown me'.

DANGER
Carcinogen
Like you didn't know

(And now a few we made up for added impact ...)

21) According to the World Health Organisation, if all of China's one billion-plus smokers lit up at the same time the resulting smog would be so thick nobody would notice what Jeffrey Archer was up to.

22) Alien abductions nearly always involve smokers. It is thought the aliens home in on the vapour trails, before beaming the victims aboard their spaceships for extensive and painful anal probing. People who smoke more than ten a day generally get gang-reamed at least twice a day.

23) Martin Gross, the inventor of
the filter tip, had a history of
making dangerous substances
a teeny bit safer. He was also
responsible for chocolate-
covered anthrax and wrapping
nuclear reactors in clingfilm
(a containment technique still
commonly used in Russia
today). He died in 1972 when
he was bitten to death by the
Rottweiler he was trying to
cover in plasticine.

You could get hit by lightning? Yeah, right. Sure

24) Passive smoking makes it 30 per cent more likely that your child will grow up gay.

25) Smoking is slavery – the
average tobacco worker toils
for seven days to collect
enough money for twenty
Rothmans while his family are
forced to roll the cigarettes on
their thighs, leading to
arthritis and premature
dementia. Also, they are forced
to eat offal ... probably.

*Jeez – 3 more
chapters to go before
another fag?
You've got to be kidding!*

*No, I'm not – now pull
yourself together, you
spineless little
prat.*

CHAPTER 4

SIMPLE QUITTING TECHNIQUES

Keep
these
lungs
tidy

These days there are literally dozens of ways to you quit. The most common is known as NRT (Nicotine Replacement Therapy) and although it is supposedly twice as likely to help you kick it is also deliberately and unnecessarily expensive.

No walking away
you big girl's blouse

Nevertheless, Quitting will eventually make you feel better and probably live longer, so it's worth knowing how effective the various techniques are, and their unlisted side effects.

Patches

Available over the counter in a variety of strengths, usually as part of a programme. The idea is to slap one on your arm every few hours until the cravings cease.

Pros – Easy to fix and forget.

Cons – Use too many and you start looking like a hypochondriac with leprosy.

You stink.
Sorry

Gum and Tablets

Available over the counter in a variety of strengths and programmes.

Pros – A direct ciggy substitute. Use when the craving is strongest.

Cons – Prolonged chewing results in a swelling of the mouth known as Coulthard's jaw.

Spray

To be used every few hours.

Pros – Supposedly very effective for casual smokers.

Cons – You look like a total bell-end … with asthma.

Bye bye

Drugs

There are several anti-smoking drugs, such as Zyban, which work by desensitizing the brain's nicotine receptors. Available on prescription only.

Pros – Very effective for heavy smokers.

Cons – Good chance you'll die while waiting for a doctor's appointment. Try one of the other methods in the meantime.

DANGER cheap lighters

Herbal Cigarettes

Widely available from herbalists.

Pros – A direct oral substitute for fags.

Cons – Often produce as much tar and carbon monoxide as real cigarettes. Also, they smell like Alan Titchmarsh's wellies.

Alternative Medicine

A wide variety of treatments, including herbal extracts, acupuncture and hypnotherapy.

Pros – Some people swear by its effectiveness.

Cons – Some people also swear that crop circles are Jesus's footprints. And do you really want some bearded git called Tarquin prodding you with needles?

Are you
gagging for a ciggy
yet? Press onto Chapter
5, which is a bit funnier,
and remember – every five
minutes without a fag is a
minor victory.
Yes it is. I'm getting paid
so I must be the expert
here.

ADVANCED QUITTING TECHNIQUES

If the obvious methods have failed, it's time to try something more radical ...

Lighting up in a known no-smoking area

For example, a swimming pool, the gym, while performing open heart surgery, during oral sex, etc.

You could get hit by lightning? Yeah, right. Sure

Spiking your ciggies

Basically, adding small amounts of dangerous substances to your filter-tipped friends. For example, spike the first one with rat poison, the second with strychnine, the third with Marmite, etc. The great benefit of this method is that it combines aversion therapy with Russian Roulette. Fancy a smoke? Well, do you feel lucky, punk?

Pulling a partner you have no hope of keeping

Find someone who is younger, richer or more attractive than yourself and persuade them to go out with you (don't ask how, this is a quitting book – pulling costs extra!). Now watch as you are forced to drop all your bad habits one by one in a futile attempt to hang on to them. Smoking is usually third on their list, after farting in bed and sleeping with their sister. Naturally, after twelve weeks of bad temper and putting on weight your new partner will dump you like toxic waste and start dating someone with a better car.

Go on,
give it a go

Become a coroner

This way you'll get to see enough blackened lungs, clotted arteries, high blood pressure and shadows on X-rays to last a lifetime. Or for a twenty-a-dayer ... about eighteen months.

Never socialize

This method lowers the possibility of temptation and prevents you buying more tobacco. It does, however, make you addicted to takeaway food and usually results in compulsory redundancy. Unless you work from home, in which case you will merely die of boredom.

Have your jaws wired together

A rare example of three vices being thwarted simultaneously: you not only smoke less but lose weight and talk rather less crap. Unfortunately, it is extremely painful and makes you sound like Brains from Thunderbirds.

Quit it! 🚭

Write a book on Quitting

Much against my will, and in order to set a good example to my readers, I now find myself three weeks into a Quitting programme. Of course, you only have my word for that, which makes it one of the more painless techniques. My own patented method goes like this:

1) Substitute your ciggies for something equally pleasurable. Currently I am cramming in around fifteen chocolate éclairs a day, but it does help.

2) Punish yourself when you do lapse (and chances are you will). The best punishment is to

---

immediately Quit again.

3) Become a rabidly
sanctimonious anti-smoker.
This increases the embarrass-
ment of failing but also makes
you something of a local
hate-figure ... which is more
fun than you might think.

See?
That had me
splitting my sides.
Anyway, if you really
really must, you can have
another ciggy now. It means
you're a pussy, but if that's
what you are then so be it.
On the other hand, who
knows the wisdom
Chapter 6 might
reveal ...

WITHDRAWAL

Bye bye

Whichever method of quitting you choose, you will certainly go through withdrawal symptoms. These differ from person to person, but drawing from my own recent experience I can confirm there are seven levels of withdrawal hell. Ironically, most people find it normal and even helpful to go through all of them – but if you can do it quicker, good on ya!

LEVEL 1

DENIAL

Symptoms: During this phase the subject denies he has Quit at all. 'Oh, that's OK,' he says, 'when I do quit not even Kylie Minogue emerging naked from the bath offering me a Silk Cut will break my resolve ... But seeing as I haven't, I might as well have another ... '

Acceptable level of failure: 1–2 ciggies

LEVEL 2

CAT WITH FIRECRACKER UP ARSE

Symptoms: OK, you've quit, and it seems to have enhanced your sensitivity to time. You look at your watch twenty times an hour, can't sit still and can't concentrate on anything for more than eight ... Oh sod it, I'm off to get some crisps!

Acceptable level of failure: Zero cigs – If you can't be arsed to make the effort, you're obviously still in Denial.

LEVEL 3

ANGER

Symptoms: You realize the true
depth of your misery and hate
everyone around you for not
appreciating the torment you're
going through. In fact, sod it –
what did they ever do for you
anyway? You deserve this fag!

Acceptable level of failure: 1 ciggy –
Go back to level 2.

LEVEL 4

HAPPY HAPPY, JOY JOY!

Symptoms: Oh my God, it's working … I can actually feel my lungs expanding. I can smell freshly mown grass. The world is my oyster and I now have the lung capacity to reach the pearl. Life is beautiful and I can't believe I didn't do this years ago!

Acceptable level of failure: Zero – Push on, this is as good as it gets.

You could get hit by lightning? Yeah, right. Sure

LEVEL 5

CONTEMPT

Symptoms: It's not that I object to you smoking in my presence – Heaven knows I used to have the odd puff myself – but think of the children! Do you really want your vile little habit corrupting their lungs and eventually turning them on to hard drugs and pornography? Well, do you?

Acceptable level of failure: Zero, plus insisting that total strangers stub out their fags immediately.

WARNING
Humourless
ex-smokers
in area

LEVEL 6

FIRST LOVE

Symptoms: It's been weeks since my last ciggy, the cravings are gone and ... hey, you know what? I'm going to have one ... just to prove how unsatisfying it is.

Acceptable level of failure: 20-plus. Level 6 is usually accompanied by a total relapse. In fact you will probably end up smoking more than you did before. Don't despair, rush on to the next level.

LEVEL 7

ACCEPTANCE

Symptoms: And finally the truth hits you. You are a junkie … a wretched worm who would crawl on your belly over dying children for one more puff.

Acceptable level of failure: Unlimited – Go back to level 1 and do it now. An immediate second Quit attempt is 15 per cent more likely to succeed than the first.

And there we are at the end of the beginning of the rest of your life. So what's it to be, smoking or non-smoking? It's make your mind up time.

(NB: If you choose smoking, you're obviously mentally subnormal and we'll give you one more try.)

CHAPTER 7

THE JAMES DEAN SYNDROME

For most of the twentieth century, smoking was cynically associated with the image of free-thinking, ass-kicking loners – the Rick Blaines, Dirty Harrys and James Bonds; people we'd all secretly like to be.

Of course, as one in two long-term smokers will die prematurely, half of them in middle age, the nonfictional ones are hacking away in heaven by now. So who were these role models and what really happened to them?

Quit it!

Contrary to popular belief, it's not all bad news. However, if all you've got in common with them is an unhealthy cough, you have to wonder whether you're picking the right qualities to emulate. Why not copy the money and gratuitous sex first, and go for the blackened lungs later? Just a thought.

You stink. Sorry

James Dean

Inventor of the syndrome and the original rebel without an ashtray. Dean smoked twenty a day, didn't care and still had the babes queuing up to snog him. Fat lot of good it did – dying after only three movies at the age of twenty-four and just as he was learning there was more to acting than pouting in a hat. But at least he got to go at 70 m.p.h. in a fast car wearing cool shades. Which is more than you can say for ...

Steve McQueen

Another heavy smoker, who this time lived to face the consequences. Curiously, he had turned into a shambling bearded semi-recluse long before being diagnosed with mesothelioma in 1979 – a form of cancer normally linked to asbestos rather than tobacco. Typically Steve … all those fags and it was still the irony that killed him.

The Marlboro Cowboy

The Marlboro Cowboy first rode onto the range in 1957, just as early medical studies linking smoking to cancer were emerging. 'I like the life a man leads out here ... ' he proclaimed. 'Like to smoke, too. My brand's MARLBORO. In my book, it's a lot of cigarette ... ' And so it was. Two of the main cowboys (Wayne McLaren and David McLean) died of cancer in the early 90s, McLean's widow allegedly maintaining he was forced to smoke up to five packs a day to look the part.

DANGER
cheap
lighters

Johnny Depp

At last! An inveterate chain-smoker who is a) still alive b) shagging gorgeous women (Kate Moss and Vanessa Paradis to name but two) and c) looking better than a smoker has a right to. How the hell does he do it, why can't we and did he really have to sign a pact with Satan to get away with it?

Bill Hicks

The thinking smoker's role model.
Overweight, sweaty, narcissistic
and still the funniest man ever to
hold a mic. 'I'm not really a heavy
smoker any more,' he once boasted,
'I only get through two lighters a
day now.' Died in 1994 of ... hmm,
let me guess.

DANGER
Harmful fumes
and dog breath

Frenchies

What is it with Frenchies and fags? We look kinda sad and desperate, they look cool and in control. Nobody smokes like Jean-Paul Belmondo, Alain Delon or Jean Reno – nobody! So what if they don't know where the soap is? France is the greatest advertisement for smoking the tobacco industry never paid for.

Now
you know the
whole truth: why you
smoke, how to quit and
what will become of you if
you don't. Still feel like
lighting up?
Damn ... blew it by
mentioning
Johnny Depp,
didn't I?

THE EMPIRE STRIKES BACK

For all the procrastinators in the house, it's time to face your true enemy. No, it's not your pitiful lack of willpower (although if you're still dying for a fag you probably deserve to).

Far more dangerous are the sinister forces committed to keeping you smoking.

The question is, do you really want people like these to win?

The tobacco industry

Not only did the tobacco industry hold out for over forty years against any claim that smoking was harmful, but top-secret files have now emerged linking it the death of JFK, the Hindenburg disaster, the Cuban missile crisis and the Roswell incident, where aliens were detained in Area 51 and forced to chain-smoke for at least a decade. We did have proof of these claims, but someone from the tobacco industry broke into my bedsit and burned it. They also stole a tenner I left on the hi-fi.

The advertising industry

Advertising has been making the unacceptable acceptable for years, usually by the use of memorable slogans. Boston copywriter Harvey Nietzbaum first came up with the slogan 'I'm not asthmatic, I'm a cowboy' in 1956, following it with the more aggressive but equally memorable 'All other brands taste like shit to me … '

As EU regulations get tougher, advertisers are moving to other means of promotion such as encouraging domestic pets to smoke and keeping Ozzy Osbourne alive for one more series.

The music industry

The music industry has always striven to keep smoking on the lips of the hip and trendy, and it started longer ago than you might think. In 1920s songwriters were working day and night on it. Who could forget such classics as 'Do the Strand' or 'A Nightingale Coughed Up in Savile Row'? Most famous of all, however, remains Jerome Kern's lesser known B-side 'Tar gets in your lungs'.

Tobacco growers

Although the majority of tobacco growers live below the poverty line while their corporate exploiters have billions in loose change to settle lawsuits, they also have a hidden agenda. Their strategy is to make Western governments feel so guilty that they legalize cocaine and marijuana and allow them to grow that instead. One tobacco grower told me: 'So we lose a couple of generations to starvation ... one day it will be our boot kicking your father's donkey, gringo!'

Quit it!

The government

Her Majesty's very own government makes at least £10 million per year off tobacco in tax and VAT – hardly an incentive to ban it. Mind you, it pays out over £1.5 billion per year via the NHS to take care of smokers, so what's the real reason it lets Formula 1 off the hook and undermines its own anti-smoking campaigns? Could it have something to do with a top-secret plan to reanimate the recently dead and use them as peacekeepers in foreign conflicts? We deserve to be told.

Boo! Hiss! What bastards! Doesn't that just make you want to Quit for good? Incidentally, if you haven't smoked since Chapter 3 treat yourself to an éclair. The rest of you read on while you can.

CHAPTER 9

THINGS YOU CAN DO BETTER AFTER YOU QUIT

No, it's not all self-sacrifice. Sure, Quitting's a pain in the butt and you will miss it like hell from time to time, but there are plenty of incentives to help you stop.

Here, for example, are some things that improve without cigarettes.

⊘ Bye bye

Sport

A no-brainer, really. Smoking reduces the lungs' capacity to absorb oxygen, as well as doing a dozen other horrible things to your heart, circulation and immune system. The reason you never saw Lynford Christie lighting up after a race is that he was busy counting the money earned from winning it. Go figure.

Sex

No, really, it's better without an ashtray propped under your partner's head – and yes, this does mean her perfume wasn't Rothman's No. 5 after all. The British Medical Association believes that over 120,000 British men are impotent because of smoking. Try blaming it on brewers' droop now.

Work

Stands to reason, really. If you're off on a fag break, you're not working. Yippee for you, but bad news for your employers, who fork out around £10 million a day to subsidize your habit.

Making money

And it's not just the bosses who lose out. At current prices, if you smoke twenty a day for twenty years you can kiss goodbye to over £32,000. For that kind of money you could hire someone to steam-clean your lungs.

Sleeping

Most people's nicotine levels drop
quickly while sleeping, one reason
we don't keep waking up every
hour for a fag. However, some
scientists (well, a couple) now
believe that sleeping smokers are
still dreaming about their habit.

For example:

Dream: You are walking down a
long white staircase. At the
bottom, you see a beautiful girl
approaching you on a unicorn,
through a field of swaying
sunflowers. She is naked.

You could get hit
by lightning?
Yeah. right. Sure

Interpretation: The staircase
represents a king-size filter-tip,
the girl is a cigarette, she is
riding a cigarette through a
field of swaying cigarettes. She
is naked because cigarettes
don't wear clothes, stupid.

WARNING
Humourless
ex-smokers
in area

Eating

Ignoring for a moment that throat cancer afflicts around seven thousand people per year (hard to swallow, eh?) how much of your last meal did you actually taste? Smoking deadens or kills taste buds and nasal receptors, resulting in one menu pretty much tasting like all the others – admittedly, a strategy which has made millions for the fast food industry.

I think I've
made my point. If
Freud taught me
anything it's that
smoking is the most evil,
vindictive, manipulative and
destructive bastard on the
planet this side of Darth
Vader's mum.
Still not convinced?

Shit!

JOKING ASIDE

As humour has patently failed to work on you, it's time to bring out the big guns; the facts.

Yes, some of them are disputed – pro-smoking groups like Forest, for instance, maintain that passive smoking kills virtually no one. However, it's up to you whether you believe that or the vast body of medical opinion. If you want to carry on smoking, at least have the guts to take responsibility. The facts don't support you, so don't try to pretend they do.

Whichever data you rely upon, the evidence is pretty conclusive that smoking is a very crap idea indeed. It's not just being linked to over fifty harmful medical conditions (twenty of which are fatal), it's the cost, social unacceptability and effect on those around you. Every year in the UK, about 120,000 people are killed by smoking (about 20 per cent of all deaths).

Quit it!

This does beg the question of why tobacco is still a legal drug and one of the government's most lucrative taxable commodities, but that's not your problem. Your problem is that if twelve million people in Britain have already quit, and 70 per cent of all smokers want to, then why can't you?

You stink.
Sorry

Here are a few valuable Web links that may help. As a firm believer in facing up to reality, I include a couple stating the opposite point of view. As with most things on the Internet, don't believe everything you read.

www.ash.org.uk An invaluable organization with links to all the support and information you could desire.

www.smokingparadise.net Ash's evil nemesis; an irreverent and defiant pro-smoking resource.

---

www.quit.org.uk Another great site, linked to Quitline (0800 00 22 00), which has already helped over two million suckers ... sorry, smokers.

www.smokingcelebs.com Yes, damnit – smoking is sexy. Not that you'll ever look as good as these guys ... with or without the ciggy.

www.cancerresearchuk.org One of many charities happy to spend some of that money you'll be saving when you Quit.

Bye bye

So there you go – we've reached the end. Feeling confident? Then all you need to complete your Quitting programme is stay off the fags and go out and buy three more copies of this book for your friends. No, don't photocopy this one, you cheap bastard – do it properly. It's called retail therapy and it's the latest thing – don't you know anything???

**DANGER
cheap
lighters**

And remember ...

1) *Don't believe the
bullshit. Smoking
is enormous fun but
Quitting is better.*
2) *Don't be afraid to fail.
Smoking a little is better
than smoking a lot.*
3) *If you do fail, Quit again
immediately. It gets easier
each time.*

Thank You for Quitting

ABOUT THE AUTHOR

Mike Anderiesz has been smoking for fifteen years. He doesn't get out enough and subsequently figures he deserves one vice. Nevertheless, for the purpose of science he has written this book alongside his second serious attempt at Quitting.

So far he has failed every day except three.

He is not discouraged. Each time he fails he starts over again and he is already down from twenty per day to five or less. He rather likes the sensation of having a daily purpose that doesn't involve making money,

You could get hit by lightning? Yeah, right. Sure

feeding his face or explaining that the reason he doesn't get enough sex is because he lacks the lung capacity to bring women down once he has tranquillized them.

Tomorrow he will quit again. He can't tell you how optimistic he feels about his chances.

No, really … he's out of breath.

TEN ABSOLUTELY IRREFUTABLE REASON[S]
TO QUIT SMOKING

- You will become rich

- You will no longer stink

- You will be more attractive to the opposite sex
  (or same sex, whatever)*

- There is nothing more satisfying than feeling smu[g]
  and who is more smug than a reformed smoker[?]

- You will be able to pass through customs witho[ut]
  the help of snide customs officials ripping throug[h]
  your luggage

- You will be able to scoff at your workmates as th[ey]
  routinely freeze outside the office every two hours [for]
  a ten-minute hit of nicotine

- You will be able to say, 'No, I don't have a spare [fag]'
  with utmost pleasure – everyone knows there's n[o]
  such thing as a spare fag

- You will be seated at the best tables in restaura[nts]

- You will have an excuse to go to the gym due [to]
  post-smoking weight gain

- You'll have more money to spend on beer; the d[rink]
  of choice for people who like to feel better abo[ut]
  themselves

www.panmacmillan.com

ISBN 0-7522-1566-3

90100

UK £2.99
$5.99 CDN

9 780752 215662

*du[e]
two [...]
give [...]